The Inventors' Club

Nicolas Brasch
Phillip Small

Australia • Brazil • Japan • Korea • Mexico • Singapore • Spain • United Kingdom • United States

The Inventors' Club

Fast Forward
Green Level 14

Text: Nicolas Brasch
Illustrations: Phillip Small
Editor: Johanna Rohan
Design: James Lowe
Series design: James Lowe
Production controller: Emma Hayes
Audio recordings: Juliet Hill, Picture Start
Spoken by: Matthew King and Abbe Holmes
Reprint: Siew Han Ong

Text © 2007 Cengage Learning Australia Pty Limited
Illustrations © 2007 Cengage Learning Australia Pty Limited

Copyright Notice
This Work is copyright. No part of this Work may be reproduced, stored in a retrieval system, or transmitted in any form or by any means without prior written permission of the Publisher. Except as permitted under the Copyright Act 1968, for example any fair dealing for the purposes of private study, research, criticism or review, subject to certain limitations. These limitations include: Restricting the copying to a maximum of one chapter or 10% of this book, whichever is greater; Providing an appropriate notice and warning with the copies of the Work disseminated; Taking all reasonable steps to limit access to these copies to people authorised to receive these copies; Ensuring you hold the appropriate Licences issued by the Copyright Agency Limited ("CAL"), supply a remuneration notice to CAL and pay any required fees.

ISBN 978 0 17 012589 5
ISBN 978 0 17 012585 7 (set)

Cengage Learning Australia
Level 7, 80 Dorcas Street
South Melbourne, Victoria Australia 3205
Phone: 1300 790 853

Cengage Learning New Zealand
Unit 4B Rosedale Office Park
331 Rosedale Road, Albany, North Shore NZ 0632
Phone: 0508 635 766

For learning solutions, visit cengage.com.au

Printed in China by 1010 Printing International Ltd
9 17

Evaluated in independent research by staff from the Department of Language, Literacy and Arts Education at the University of Melbourne.

THE Inventors'

Nicolas Brasch
Phillip Small

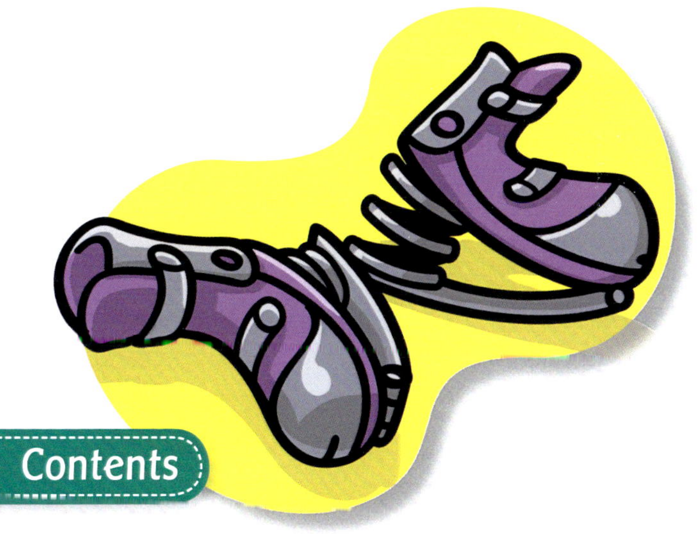

Contents

Chapter 1

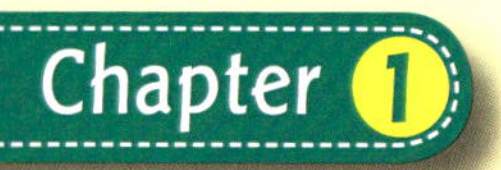

The Third Thursday of Every Month

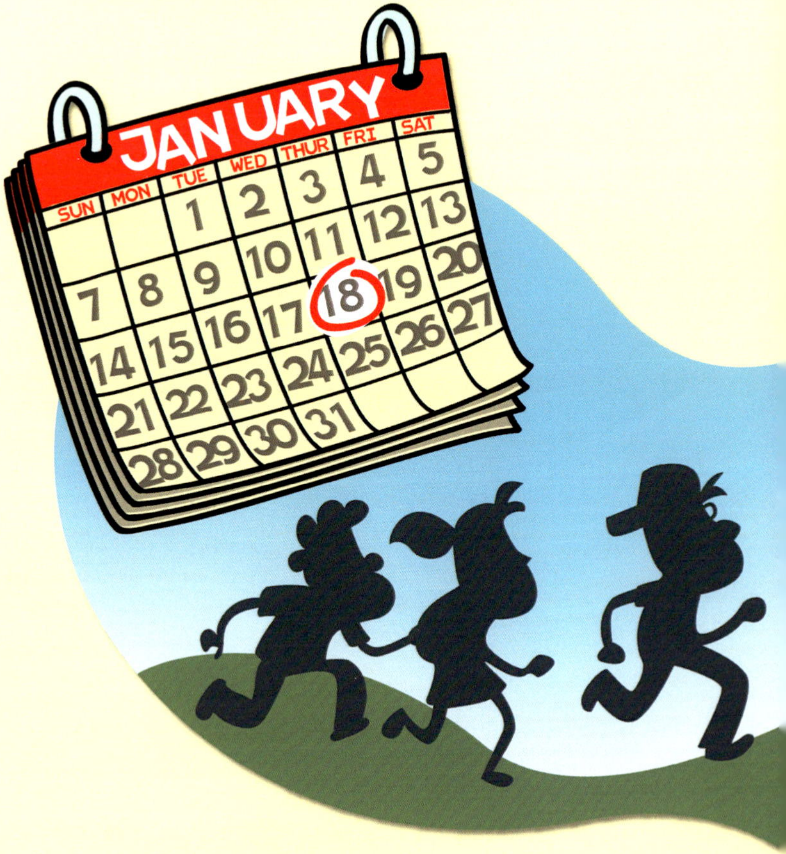

The Inventors' Club met
on the third Thursday of every month.
Their meetings were top secret.

Chad, Ben, Bianca and Jodie raced from school to Chad's house for the meeting of the Inventors' Club.

At each meeting,
one of the inventors showed
all the others an invention
they had made.

Each inventor
took it in turn
to invent something.

Chapter 2

Bianca's Invention

Last Thursday, the inventors were sitting in Chad's bedroom.

Bianca sat in the corner.
She put on some basketball shoes.

Chad, Ben and Jodie watched her.
It was Bianca's turn
to show off her invention.

Bianca stood up
when she had put on the shoes.

"What's so special about
your basketball shoes?"
laughed Chad.

"Just wait and see," said Bianca.

Chapter 3

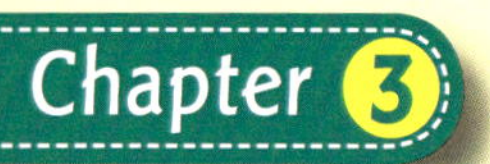

"Goal!"

"Just pretend I'm playing basketball," Bianca said.

Then she started running around
the bedroom,
pretending to bounce a ball.

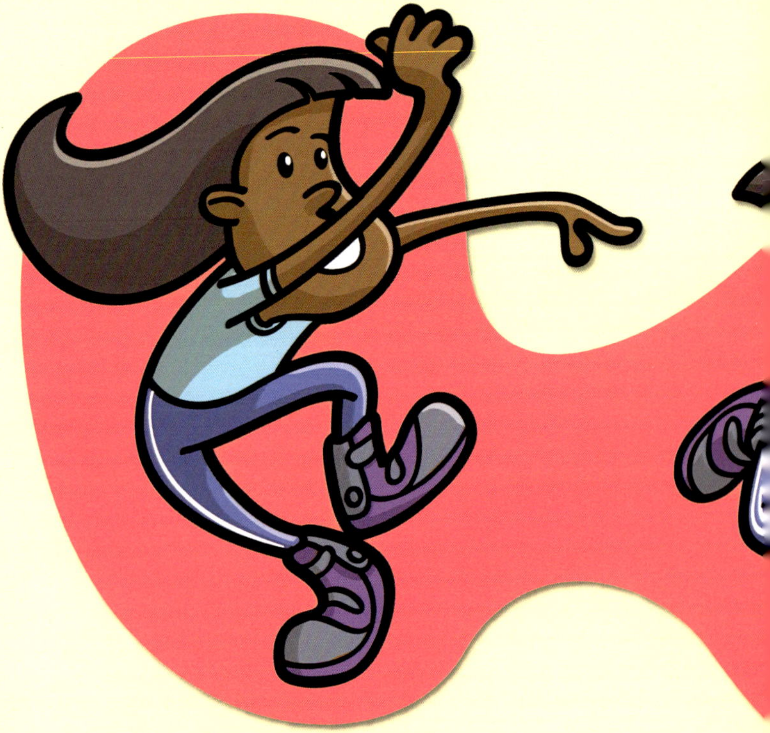

"I'm coming to the hoop,"
Bianca yelled.
"I've got players on my left
and players on my right.
I go for the hoop!"

Running Words 161

Bianca acted out
what she was saying.

"Then I leap into the air ...
Goal!" she yelled.
The others could not believe how high
Bianca leapt into the air.

"Goal!"

Bianca sat down
and took off the shoes.
She showed the others the springs
that were glued to the bottom
of them.

The shoes had springs,
which made Bianca leap high
into the air.

"That's a great invention," said Jodie.

One Second to Go

"Let me have a go," said Ben.

"They won't work on you,"
Bianca told him.

"Yes, they will.
If you can make them work,
I sure can," said Ben.

“I made them for someone my size,”
Bianca said.
“You will be too heavy.”

Ben grabbed the shoes.

Ben squeezed his feet
into the basketball shoes.
It was a tight fit,
but he was able to put them on.

Then he stood up and started to act
like a basketball player,
just like Bianca.

"There's three seconds left,"
yelled Ben.
"We're a point down.
I rush to the hoop
with two seconds to go.
I leap in the air
with one second to go!"

Ben leapt into the air ...

Chapter 5

"Help Me!"

Ben went higher and higher.
He was heading for the open window.

Ben yelled and waved his arms,
but it didn't help.

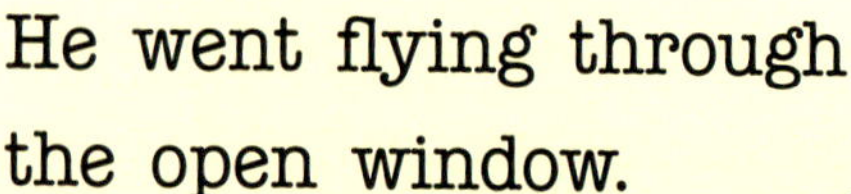

He went flying through
the open window.

The others ran to the window
and looked outside.
Ben was hanging on to a tree,
high above the ground.

"Help me!" he yelled.

The others just laughed and laughed.

"I said you would be too heavy," Bianca told Ben.

"I guess you didn't win the game!" Jodie yelled to Ben.

"Just help me get down from here!" Ben yelled.